PLATINUM BLONDE

Phoebe Stuckes is a writer from West Somerset now based in London. She has been a winner of the Foyle Young Poets award four times and is a former Barbican Young Poet. She has performed at the Southbank Centre, Waterstones Trafalgar Square and Wenlock Poetry Festival, and was Ledbury Poetry Festival's young poet in residence in 2015. She has also read her work on BBC Radio 3. Her writing has appeared in *The Poetry Review*, *The Rialto*, *The North*, and *Ambit* among others. Her debut pamphlet, *Gin & Tonic* (smith | doorstop, 2017) was shortlisted for the Michael Marks Award 2017, and she won an Eric Gregory Award in 2019. Her first full-length collection, *Platinum Blonde*, was published by Bloodaxe in 2020. A poem from the book, 'Thus I became a heart-eater', won the Poetry Society's Geoffrey Dearmer Prize 2019.

PHOEBE STUCKES

Platinum Blonde

BLOODAXE BOOKS

Copyright © Phoebe Stuckes 2020

ISBN: 978 1 78037 502 1

First published 2020 by
Bloodaxe Books Ltd,
Eastburn,
South Park,
Hexham,
Northumberland NE46 1BS.

www.bloodaxebooks.com
For further information about Bloodaxe titles
please visit our website and join our mailing list
or write to the above address for a catalogue

Supported using public funding by
ARTS COUNCIL
ENGLAND

Cover design: Neil Astley & Pamela Robertson-Pearce.

Printed in Great Britain by Bell & Bain Limited, Glasgow, Scotland, on
acid-free paper sourced from mills with FSC chain of custody certification.

I'm a red hot fox
I can take the knocks
I'm a hammer from hell
oh honey can't you tell?
I'm the wild one.

SUZI QUATRO, MIKE CHAPMAN

ACKNOWLEDGEMENTS

These poems or earlier versions of them have appeared in the following publications: 'Gold Hoop Earrings' and 'Thus I became a heart-eater' in *The Poetry Review*; 'Three Spells' in *Ambit*; 'Crisis' in Rising; 'Ghosts' in the *Wenlock Poetry Festival Anthology 2016*; 'Advice for Girls' online as a commended winner of the Troubadour Prize; 'Imminent Catastrophe' in *An Orchestra of Feather and Bone*, the Barbican Young Poets Anthology 2017; 'Lying' in *Hwaet! 20 Years of Ledbury Poetry Festival* (Bloodaxe Books/Ledbury Poetry Festival, 2017); 'Supermoon' and 'Sun Sign' in *The Kindling*; 'Kiss me quick' in *Ash*; '$$$' in *The Rialto*; 'Home', 'Judgement' and 'Crisis' in *Introduction X: The Poetry Business Book of New Poets* (2017); 'Bad Girls Club', 'Francesca Woodman', '*Carrie* (1976)' and 'Mad Chicks Cool' in The Poetry Archive.

'Cassandra' was originally commissioned by the *Bedtime Stories for The End of The World* podcast. Several poems appeared in *Gin & Tonic*, a smith|doorstop pamphlet published by The Poetry Business in 2017.

Endless thanks is due to the Foyle Young Poets Award and the Poetry Society for their support of my work from a young age. To Jacob Sam-La Rose, R.A Villanueva and all the Barbican Young Poets for always renewing my enjoyment of poetry. To Harry Man, Jack Underwood and Eva Salzman for their invaluable workshops and editorial help. To my Mum and Dad and my siblings Dominic and Imogen. And to the following people for their support and poetic guidance: Dominic Hale, Jack Wrighton, Emily Meller, Maria Carranza, Joshua Judson and most of all to Catriona Bolt.

CONTENTS

Bleach

I liked the blonde but it was too powerful,
I had to grow it out, my head was a hot white coal

in the night. Men loved me too much,
they followed me on foot or in their slick cars,

at a slow pace, saying nothing.
I could hear the slow grind of their wheels

or their heavy footsteps, out of tune with the timbre
of my stilettos. I wasn't wearing stilettos

but I think you will imagine that I was.
When I picked up one of those shoes in Topshop

my mother said, you'll break your ankle
and I did not believe her. She said, you'll come unstuck

and I did. These days I keep my feet firmly laced
to the earth, in trainers, I'm always ready to run.

Carrie (1976)

Have you ever seen
a woman in a plastic tiara throw up?

I have been her, dressed up
as *Carrie*, straight men and dogs

licking the fake blood from my arms.
I think it was the man with his face

painted up as a skeleton
who spiked my gin and tonic.

He could have wrapped his hand around
my upper arm as I unlocked my door.

I try not to imagine anything. I go
where I please but I'm being hunted.

I'm running as fast as I can
to the end of this year. The new one

trawls in like a married man and his shadow
eats mine on the pavement.

Supermoon

Life is full of nightmares that are enormous and dark
like whales. Sometimes it's like standing at the side

of the highway doing nothing, others it's like
dodging speeding trucks. I get older but I still get

everything wrong. I still trip on my shoes and take
pills I find in the carpet. I think everyone I've slept with

is precious and important. I want to call them all up
and hold them against my chest like a bundle of daffodils.

It takes a serious heft of my self control
not to run through the streets barefoot every day,

or walk into the ocean and let her take me.
This is how I want to die: in a boat, on fire

while Billie Holliday crawls out of a speaker.
I want everyone to be watching.

Three spells

Lost boys, go home
I like my boring life.
I'm hard as silver
and you are a fleshy blood thing.
Get out of my hands
and my inbox.

Mother deliver me from gin headaches,
I've lost enough Sunday mornings
as it is. I've written enough
thank you notes and apology letters
now is the time
for manifestos and songs.

Girl, have a peppermint tea
and sleep on it.
Keep hold of your story
like a dog on a lead.
Trust me, you'll burn through
these months like sage.

Monologue

I'm not shivering.
Once this breeze drops, I'll be fine.
Give me two Paracetamol and a week,
I can't face another doctor,
another cul-de-sac. I'm not going back

to my parents'. I can't remember
what I used to be like or what I did yesterday.
I'm sorry I kept your book for so long
I'm sorry I met you and flirted,
but never phoned or

texted back. Buy me another
and I'll take you home, I'll make you
believe in the sound of your voice
in the movement of your hands.
Other people's insecurities are so

romantic. I've not worked on my essays
but I'm going out anyway.
This dress makes me feel
like I could be loved. I'm starving
for something. Kebab shop chips

or a gin and tonic.
I'm wilting in this heat like blossom.
I'm turning the corner
to another accident and emergency.
I could hurt myself but I probably won't.

Platinum Blonde

On those days I get enamoured with my face
or an outfit. I remember the year every girl
wore a garland of flowers and it became
a negative thing. Everyone hates a whimsical girl.

They don't find themselves funny but men do,
with their plain clothes and serious thoughts.
That summer I tried to be like them, I was always
on my way to another funeral, clad in black

and hiking boots. I made fun of the funny
whimsical girls. Now I'd die to be with them.
Sometimes I dream my eyeliner
goes all the way up to my ears like spiders' legs.

Before prom I glued lashes to my eyes
that were heavy and forced them half shut.
My brother laughed but I didn't think
it was funny. The last time my heart broke

I bleached my hair and sat in the salon chair
with my scalp blistering like guilt. That night
I slept alone on an empty living room floor. I can laugh
about it now but I don't think it was funny.

Bad Girls Club

How could you really know yourself
if you'd never had that fake hair extension

ripped from the back of your head,
in the car park of the big Tesco

some time in the Spring of 2010,
the scrap of synthetic lace in your thighs

already stained with blood, already
too fat for your cutoffs, and a girl

called Jessie, the most frightening
and gorgeous being you had ever seen.

Kiss me quick

When I think a boy is beautiful
I feel like Frank O'Hara, crooning
over St Sebastian in his orange shirt.

Everyone I want is stuck with arrows.
My first kiss came immediately
after I quit church, I knew

I was going to hell for it and then I did.
I never cried so much in my life.
I don't know how to avoid

gorgeous men. There is always
another one and I always love him.
I can't stop producing bouquets

from my empty sleeves.
I am wearing all these poems
to the wedding disco.

I am meeting someone
in the middle of the dance floor,
oh god, I hope it's not you.

Hell is a bus full of the men I have unsuccessfully tried to love –

all of them saying no, or worse,
saying nothing at all, getting taller

and more devastating like black clouds.
When I look down the barrels of their eyes

in their profile pictures, I can see
where I have been buried.

I was fourteen and the thinnest I have ever been
when a boy told me I shouldn't have cut my hair

because he told me not to. I will do anything
to avoid being abandoned by my mother

at the supermarket, I don't feel worthy of love
when my false eyelash starts to come off,

or when I consider the backs of my thighs
in the ladies loo, in the back of the restaurant.

Perhaps this is a feminine problem, like cystitis
or fathers. All of us are apologising

and taking antibiotics, but we daren't ask
for anything like could someone please

take down all these mirrors? Or when I die
will the photos of me naked on your phone be deleted?

Advice for Girls

Vanilla-based perfumes drive men wild,
we have no evidence for this. Sudocrem
is good for spots, cuts, grazes, rashes
and sadness. Always accompany your friend
to the clinic. Boyfriends cannot be trusted
in this matter. Eyebrows are sisters not twins,
let this knowledge free you. Get a hot water bottle
for period pain, buy your own chocolate,
boyfriends cannot be trusted in this matter.
Nail varnish can be used to stop tights laddering,
if your tights ladder you cannot keep wearing them,
no it is not *Punk*. Get someone to help when dyeing
your hair, blot your lipstick. Don't borrow mascara
from women you don't trust. Text me when you get home,
keep your hand on the door in the back of the taxi.
I found his Facebook, I'm friends with his sister's
best friend's zumba instructor. Dairy makes you fat,
gluten is evil but we don't know how or why or what it is.
Beyoncé, Beyoncé, Beyoncé.

Sugar

I have accidentally loved
several rich girls. When I found out
one was dating some boy wonder
rock star, as well as me, I considered
lifting some art from her parents'
walls and starting a better life
in a new city. I could never
have a sugar daddy because I don't
look after myself. I chew at my own
fingers and lick knives at dinner,
there is an inch of brown hair
on my head that is eating
the blonde, like a snake
I am shedding my old self. I used
to say money didn't matter
now I would give anything
to be wrapped up in cash like a thick
fur coat on my naked body. If you must cry
it's better to do so in the back of a Bentley.

Marshmallows

Devotion is overrated, what am I supposed to do
with something so temporary? I guess I wouldn't know.

Is it like being given a cheese by someone you love?
Once you've eaten it all, what's left? Dry crackers,

commitment? Suzanne Mallouk said
Jean-Michel Basquiat bought her bags of pink

and white marshmallows when he had no
money for cakes. I cried on the megabus

where I read this, thinking of the crepe I bought
for the girl I loved at the time, knowing I would

never have the money to fly out
and see her after she had gone home.

Blood

November's hands are warm.
He has a girlfriend but says, if he didn't

things would be different. It is always
this way, he says he is painfully attracted

to me. I should throw down my glass
and leave but I won't, I have to be ordered out

like a dog and wouldn't I rather be loved?
Wouldn't I rather get up every morning

in the sunshine and be dressed
by songbirds? He doesn't want me,

he wants to look at me, behind glass
he wants me to reach out and smear blood

but not so it gets on his clothes, not so
it's still visible when he gets home.

Stronger than me

I knew something was wrong
because he watched horror movies

in the middle of the day, while he ate his sandwiches.
The last time we met, the sky cracked up

like wet unvarnished wood. We agreed,
thunderstorms are like crying hard.

I hit him with my umbrella's broken wings
and stuffed it in a dustbin. Each morning I had to

walk down the road he took away from me.
He lived above a funeral director's, I thought about

dying in his flat, all the time, and once stole
a razor blade from his bathroom

which is the sort of funny story I would
have told him, if it wasn't about him.

Cassandra

1

I know a bad boy when I see one,
the problem is I want to cradle
their heads in my lap. I think I need
a big strong man to take care of me,

but when one arrives I can't stop
screaming. Sometimes desire has
nothing to do with you, it just gets
angled towards your shape.

I expect to come to a sticky end.
Lately I imagine myself strangled to death
on a velvet banquette, my fishnets ripped
and my eyes rolled back to the whites.

Shall I work backwards?
The man who almost dissolved me
had a seventies porn star moustache
and this didn't seem like a problem.

After it happened,
I locked myself in the bathroom.
There was a strange girl in the mirror,
I think I left her there.

Now, on dates I list my fears,
cephalopods, the dentist,
those men who want women to act like dogs.
The past never stays where you put it.

Last week I heard him laughing
from the other side of an empty shopping centre.
I lost three days. He liked my body
too much, now I want it to go.

When I think of what I eat
I feel like a seabird filled with plastic.
I wish you could see all the way through me
like the fish that live their whole lives in total darkness.

2

Hundreds of years ago
I was drowned in a pond
for exactly the same reasons.
A piece of glass

lives under my pelvis,
lodged since childhood
already cracked open.
Shall I work backwards?

3

Where did I get these green and yellow flowers at my wrists?
This handful of violets at my throat?
Why is my bottom lip swollen?
I said no didn't I? Did I say no this time?

4

Mad girl starts driving the bus.
I put my feet up on the dashboard.
Mad girl says how much
for a baseball bat?

She says flat shoes
she says keys in the knuckles
she says door locked from the inside
she says check the wardrobe

check under the bed. Mad girl says
can you walk me home
please can you walk me home
can you stay on the line while I walk home?

Mad girl says he is not real anymore
but I am. She says he's pretty mouthy
for a hallucination. She says this is my house,
she says are you scared? What are you a ghost?

You don't know shit about being dead,
I have been dead.
Have you ever sunk your hands
into the silt at the bottom of the pond?

I have been there.

Mad girl says it wasn't my fault
Mad girl says it was never my fault.
She says it doesn't matter
if you believe me

she says I'd chip his name off
the granite next to yours
with my fingernails
if I had to.

Mad girl says half of you wouldn't know
a wolf if it had its jaws around
your ankle, wolves come in all shapes
and sizes, that's why you set traps.

Mad girl says she's wolf-proof.

AWOOOOOOOOOOO AWOOOOOOO
OOOOOOO AWOOOOOOOOOOO

Mad girl says I wouldn't have survived
any other time. I would've died
of consumption, childbirth,
cotton in the lungs, boredom,

strangled with my own petticoat.
They would've had us
lobotomised.
She says we're lucky.

5

Mad girl says they're going to come here,
with their torches and pitchforks.
The lawyers, the questions, the cops,
the bastards, they will never stop coming.

They will come here, the wives
standing up for their husbands.
They will pour the molten gold
of their wedding rings down your throat

if you let them. Do not let them.

6

Mad girl is always correct
though she is rarely heard.
She talks and talks, she talks
until she screams. Until she talks

until she starts again.

7

Did he put his hands straight
through you like smoke?
Did it snap something in you
like thread?

Are you carrying it on your back
like a whole other person?
Is the deadweight of his name
sticking in your throat?

Do they ask you if you know him?
Has he kept you that secret?
Are you supposed to have evidence?
Could you point to where the pain is?

Could you tell him
he did this? If you saw him,
could you run? If you saw him,
could you run? If you saw him?

8

Watch me.
This is the noise I make when kicked.

I'm high up on my thunder thighs.
I used to be slender as a thought,

now he'd tremble to pass me on the street,
as he should. He'd have to cut me in half

to lift me up. I have come back
to pester the living, to show them the ways

they have failed me. My eyes
are the quiet centre of the hurricane,

the voice on the other end of the line
is his own cry for help and it says

you have to live with me,
the way I live with you.

Gold Hoop Earrings

Someone did this to me, I loved him
but that doesn't matter. Having an affair

is just getting all dressed up to cut yourself.
My brain used to shut itself off and go quiet

and fuzzy, the moment he put his hands
on me or took them off. I've tried to imagine

how he felt but I was too busy falling down
my own set of drains. I'm going to spend my life

correcting his attraction to me. I'm different now.
I'll never wear lingerie again. I'm going to acquire

some gold hoop earrings and find someone
to film me talking and talking. I am going

to leave the country, and become
an impressive nightmare, just watch me.

Forgiveness

Sometimes I think about the flat and him
inside of it. His hands like rats, my chest

a cutting-board beneath him. The word *no*
was short for nothing there. I shook like thunder

for weeks afterwards. I used to think love
was a smashed glass and a trickle of blood.

There are things I was taught as a child
that I still believe now. In all probability

someone did to him what he did to me in another
time. But that doesn't necessarily help either of us.

Why does he do that

Sometimes men are angry because
they don't know which room in the house
to lock you in. Sometimes men are angry

because you said *men*, because you can
see them, because you have thrown them
against a pale background. Sometimes men

are angry because they don't know what
to do with their hands. Sometimes your man is
angry for no reason at all, you just see him

trapped in a hurricane of his own making
and if you try to stick your hands in it
to hold his, he will take them off you.

Fear

Of being trapped

At night I dream about him methodically
plugging my mouth with cotton wool balls,

moving from the right cheek to the left,
building a hillock of quiet.

Of abandonment

At night I dream about him leaving
and then he does.

Of intimacy

At night I dream we are talking it through
as he connects the metal poles

for a temporary gazebo.
I wake up and we never do.

Wolfish

1

Once he said white cats
were doe-eyed flirts
and stared at me
as he pushed her little head
down with his knuckles

2

His mother said red roses
were slutty, my arms
are full of them

3

I turned his skin green
where I held him
like cheap gold rings

Home

If I'm left alone
I get swamped by the urge
to cut off my hair
or dye it an unnatural colour
one-handed, in the sink.

I want to wear black
but getting dressed feels
like being stood up.
I've a date with nothing,

I'm swallowing endless photos
of exes in foreign countries
or at festivals. I suffocate my heart
in pasta and cheese sauce,
leave the dishes submerged

in rock pools of soap.
If I google how to know
if you're having a breakdown
the links are all purple.
Outside, seagulls are hooting

like ambulances.
I don't trust myself enough
to open an upstairs window
to watch them wheeling around.

Blues

I'm usually on my way to the library
or another hospital.

Filling in a questionnaire,
or watching the clock

for my appointment.
I've been mad for years.

I retain the ability to text
and go on the internet.

On most days I can feed myself;
stir tomatoes around a frying pan,

wind spaghetti around a fork.
Though the dishes can go untouched for weeks.

Sometimes I can even go out of the flat
and walk down the street.

It will be summer soon, only
a matter of time before I fall

for someone else unavailable.
My mother thinks I should come home

at the weekends.
Perhaps I should get more exercise

Perhaps I should get diagnosed.
You don't know what I've done in the small hours.

You don't know
what I've done to cope.

$$$

If I could stay out of trouble
for more than five minutes
I could crack the heavens

but I'm too busy falling. I have bled
on the duvet covers of several handsome
and moderately successful men.

This is not when I most feel like a woman,
that comes later, in the bathroom
of the walk-in centre as I push a pristine

cotton bud into my cunt and return it
to the receptionist in its plastic coffin.
I have to leave London, everyone

is trying to kill me or get me pregnant.
I used to think I had conditions, now
it seems I'm free to anyone. I'm showered

with broken windows. I lean over in the gutter
and vomit wads of cash. So broke
I stink of pennies. I am ruined.

Attempt

This is what I remember: the paramedic said
we can't help you unless you've already died,
we have to know you are serious. I think his name

was Dennis, I said it feels pretty *fucking* serious Dennis.
I thought death might render me serene but it didn't.
I wasn't going down without a fight. I wanted to steal

the backless cotton nightgown they gave me to wear.
It was soft, and pink, I wanted to shove it in my handbag
and run. As usual, I cried all my makeup off. I flirted

with the junior doctor. He said I had *young woman's*
syndrome, which means your veins are hard to find.
I said, you have no idea, and puked. My head split

all the way along its seams, it took my mother an age
to arrive. When they sent her out she did not go,
she hung around all night. I did not die.

Look at me now

Talking about it
is like trying
to recover

a dead language.
There is nowhere
I can point to

on my body.
The clothes I wore
have been bagged up

and thrown out.
I am still married
to your likeness,

I find you
serving cookies
in Paddington Station,

ordering drinks
in New Cross Inn.
A strand of hair,

an eyelash is enough
to reduce me to panic.
I am recovered,

like a mermaid
washed up on land.
Integrated

into a standing,
talking society.
If I could, I would

draw a line as long
as four years.
Look how far

I have walked
from where you left me.
Look at me now,

sleeping with other people.
Laying down
with the enemy,

encouraging them
to touch me
in all the same ways

you did, never once
allowing them
to walk me back home.

Fox

I'm usually hanging around
in dressing gowns.
Buttering toast and calling a friend
to complain about poetry
or the government.

It's a rough time to be young
or to care about anything.
So I keep wandering through London
looking for something to do.

I rattle around these streets
like an urban fox.
In my second-hand fur
eating junk out of polystyrene.

I don't like to follow
the thick grey artery that leads
to my flat, where I live with myself.
I tell myself that crying in cabs

could be glamorous
if I did it correctly.
I am doing my best
with bad nights and bad love.
Honey it's difficult.

Disco

Last new moon in Scorpio I coughed up blood
two days later met another man he was

so much stronger than me sooner or later
I pay for everything I do my beloved will not

come back anytime soon though I carry her name
like a silver dollar in my mouth oh I am dying

for something gold-plated for something
as old-fashioned as marriage I wish someone

would buy my shoes for me but expect nothing else
I will not shave my legs or pretend to appreciate

TV shows in which women are violently murdered
I could overlook the inconsistencies and rape scenes

but I'm in my early twenties a party girl
running low on favours

my life is already like that
I don't need to watch it on screen

Bronski Beat

This boy thinks it's 1986
he's staying in the club
until it closes for fear of going back

home to a nuclear winter to a flat
with the power cut off he says
the meth only made his hands go numb

it never tracked its way to his heart
I never found it either he never
used condoms with men or women

like me this boy he thinks he's already
dead he thinks he's slipped the bouncer
talked his way into paradise

Romance

He excites me the same way that Death does like
when Death gets here do you think he will pay for drinks

do you think he'll touch my thigh under the table
I can get giddy and romantic I lock loving eyes

with taxi drivers as they speed towards me they never
slow down I have to be hauled out of the road

by the strong arms of my male friends before we fall in love
I want to know if you would murder me and how

would you finish the job would they ever find my body
would they know it was you always you my love it was always you

Sun Sign

His mother calls him honey,
I want to call her and say
you did your best. Your son

has many good qualities
and I like him. I like him
with the dismal hope of a dog

begging for chocolate.
I have read a lot of literature
on whether our star signs

are compatible. The consensus is
that the connection is magnetic
when mutual, but of course, it never is.

I know your ex-husband is a Pisces
because your son said, my dad is a Pisces,
what are Pisces people like? I held him

and said in my experience, they will always
hold your hand in public but the minute
you are out of sight, they disappear.

Scorpion

I want to text him this picture of a woman
with a scorpion tattooed on her breastbone.

He likes this sort of thing: pain and long term
consequences. I would never do it but I like

the idea of something spiky and black
stamped somewhere private and soft,

like my inner thigh, a scorpion
threatening my cunt with its tail.

Sext

(after Richard Siken)

I want to tell you this story without saying I liked him.
Without saying it was me, running late to work or hiding
in the bathroom. Listening to clips of his voice saying

I want to bite down on the soft part of your neck
and never let go never never let go. I want to tell you
I don't imagine myself, buckling underneath that first kiss,

against the kitchen sink. I want to tell you I didn't say
kill me when I was lying on the sofa. Without saying
the words were meant for another man, another sofa,

another failure to get the little life out of my throat.
I want to tell you his hip bone didn't leave a bruise
on my thigh as large and dark as an ultrasound photograph.

I want to tell you it didn't take a month to disappear.

BDSM

When he hits you it's as if
it's happening to someone else.

Even though you asked him to do it
your chest flutters like a birds

as you try to crawl backwards,
and he pulls you towards him.

This is the feeling you wanted,
of being pulled towards. You want

to hold his face in your hands
for a long time, searching

his dark eyes for sweetness.
For the reflection of yourself, always

diminishing, your chest shuddering,
your hands coming down on yourself.

How to get over it

You must do something drastic. Pierce your ears,
name the studs after those who've hurt you.
When they get infected, cleanse with sea salt

and fury. Start wearing heels and bras again,
when you remember pain, give up. Fuck a friend
whose ex-girlfriend you love and admire.

Believe you are pregnant; eat half a tub
of ice cream and puke. Resent the friend,
resent the child, decide to stop speaking

to everyone you know. Discover
the child is imaginary, love the single line
on the test like it is your own life.

Meet a handsome doctor at the new surgery
and really, really hate him.

Proposal

I'm reading on the steps outside a chapel
I tell you I'm hoping to meet a nice Christian boy
do you know any who might be interested
in saving me and you say
literally dozens

don't men want an impossible task
a hostile land to die in something
to whimper over during the winter evenings
I could be that for someone
my love I could be that for you

Ghosts

Lately I've been getting to know
the ghosts in your kitchen.
Mostly when you're answering emails
or deep in conversation with the cat.

By the counter, one strums your guitar,
one picks up your favourite books,
flicks through, and drops them.
Drums her nails on the table

you re-painted yourself.
By the window, one is applying
red lip gloss to her mouth and pouting.
This one is covered in hairpin scars

and tends to keep you up past twelve
with work in the morning, with a noise
like a siren, that never quite leaves you alone.
This is where they prefer to congregate

and talk, though of course
they can walk through walls.
One plaits my hair, one says
I don't know you like they do.

Your kitchen is crowded, imagine
that many birthdays to remember,
so many phone numbers pinned
to a small board.

Wet

Is it too late to tell you
this is what love looks like sometimes
I am holding the name of the girl in my mouth

like gum in church I am holding the name of the girl
who opened you up like a scallop with a knife
I want to use my hands to hold your wet insides

sometimes this is what love looks like I am holding
her name in my mouth like a cough sweet
and it numbs me all the way down

Dinner

I have chewed my lip bloody
trying not to be in love with you.

I wear all the marks of the wounded,
the soft grey jumper, the ringless fingers.

I've cried about you in every major
fast food chain, and on all my bus routes.

Today I realised our miseries are
incompatible. I cannot blame

how I told you I have crawled into bed
with a box of chips – or the few

occasions you have seen me naked –
for why we are not together.

How could I have known
you were expecting to chase

my sadness off? Or when you couldn't
we would stop having dinner?

That final time was enough to ruin
my favourite restaurant, which is one

of three things I cannot forgive you for.
The second is putting ketchup

on your mac and cheese, the third is burning
my house down and leaving me in it.

A good man is a humane mouse-trap

I think often of the good men.
The men who knew when to stop.
Who knew me so well,
they knew what I wanted

right up until they didn't.
The men who said they were sorry.
The good men have cried with me,
called me, they have wanted

to know how I got home.
These men couldn't believe
what other men had done,
but they nodded anyway.

The good men try their hardest.
They have never loved me
but they have liked me,
very much. These men

love their girlfriends,
their wives. The good men
enjoy my angry poems,
so secure are they in the knowledge

that they were not written
about them. My mother raised me
on tales of these good men,
she is very sure of their existence.

The good men are out there.
I just need to catch and marry one
quickly, before the bad ones find out
where I've been hiding.

Kissing a girl in front of the Salvation Army church

like leaning out of the kitchen window to flip off God
like burning a fainting couch like an obscenity trial like cutting
a string of pearls like punching a Manet like ripping a sticker
off a bathroom door like wearing satin flares to a funeral
like pretending to forget your ex's name like growing pansies
in the desert like falling in love then paying for it

Daughter

When I was young I was so good I was St Lucia
three years running. My mother crowned me

with lit candles wrapped in tin foil, I couldn't
protest because I was the vicar's daughter.

I had to stand and proclaim my sainthood
wick-straight and pray I wouldn't go up in flames.

Thus I became a heart-eater

I was holding myself like an open flame
at Candlemas, when the doughnut
presented itself: glossy red and obscene.

The same vague heart-shape
of a woman's face. I ate it
in three bites, in the street, thinking

of Valentine's Day, how every year
it manages to hurt my feelings. How
when I was young I wanted to be called

Valentine, the bringer of love. How
I used to want a minute black heart tattooed
on my buttock, where only a lover could find it,

and what would be the point of that, now?
Then I swallowed and sucked the sugar
from my fingers, like a disgusting child at a fair.

Purple Heart

My ex's aura is bright red and mine is blue
or violet or vantablack disappearing dark
and taking all the light with it I want to call her
on the phone and listen to her describe things
beaches in Oregon her new girlfriend on roller skates
the weather the only way to fall out of love
is to write poems like this as your heart leaks poisonously
into your chest like hotel shampoo into a suitcase
like you I am wondering if I will always be like this

Francesca Woodman

I see my face in everything
perhaps this is my biggest flaw

to always be catching glimpses
dishevelled in car windows shop fronts

the bathrooms of restaurants
Narcissus is a white nodding flower

I'm just self obsessed I wonder if I stare
hard enough I might metamorphosize

into another girl slender a bushel of
brown hair over my shoulder powdering

myself with flour or laying down sweetly
with a basket of eels or if like her one morning

short of money and love I might push
my apartment windows wide and step out

Pangea

Always breaking up/just broke up with someone/
broken up about it/in pieces/heart-broken/*who did it*
I'll kick their teeth in/yes I am/broken/
heart-aching/cutting myself/trying to pick it up/
yes I am too much/foolish/cleaning broken
glass up/wrong/broke a window trying to get into
the house I used to live in/now/I have/nowhere/to go

Poem in which I leave and don't come back

What do I do without you? Love,
I go to work. I let the hole you made in my tights

with your thumbnail grow out like mould.
I fold napkins, mop chemicals into ampersands

on the floor. The milk jugs are my favourite,
they look like miniature birds, chirping against

each other on the circular tray. Dropping them
would be almost as bad as bursting into tears,

I could break most of them in an instant. If you're a bird,
then I'm one too, we can either mate for life
or get sucked into a wind turbine.

Lying

I think of tattoos like love or childbirth:
if it were that painful, everyone would stop.
We could get by on goldfish and biros,
squares of wax paper that sponge on a mark.
I don't believe that everything worthwhile
takes commitment. Takes waiting rooms
and what must be foolishness. Take this girl,
first doodled by Picasso on a napkin
maybe, then drawn into my arm with needles
one bent-up Wednesday. She reminds me of you,
how you clutched my hand in the clinic, your nails
digging into my palms, before the nurse came
to take you away. How we both say that it hurt
and anyone who says otherwise is lying.

Is this thing on?

I don't want to write about death
anymore. I'm tired of always taking off
my heels and crying on the steps
outside the ballroom. I want to stuff
the whole sky in my mouth like
an Hermès scarf, like candy floss
from a plastic bucket. I want to
submissively drink the blood
from your neck, in the early evening,
Gorgeous I'm starving.

Confessional

Baby you are not always as right as you think you are
but you know I must be very hard up to want love

in this economy of shop floors and polishing dinner knives
holding their excruciating heat in a dry cloth napkin

in my chapped hands in this climate of all my not inconsiderable
emotions for no money where all my blood couldn't buy me

a yellow silk skirt why would I ask the devil for love
why am I trying to give away everything I have

am I more religious than I thought should I go to Rome
or worse am I trying to disappear am I covering myself up

with soil or strips of wallpaper
why would I ask for love when I could curl up

around a thick fur coat when like a cat I will curl up in warmth
from just about anywhere why then would I ask you for love

Mad Chicks Cool

A mad chick is a bloodstain on a white skirt.
She has no mother of her own but gave birth
to herself in a shell or a dustbin. Every time

you cut off the head of a mad chick, two more
sprout in her place. Men want to fuck us
but wouldn't spit on a mad chick if she

were on fire. Right now, a mad chick
is cosying up to your girlfriend on a velvet
chaise longue. Your new boss is a mad chick,

perhaps your mother was a mad chick
which is why you hate them now. Watch out,
the mad chicks are in the street outside,

ripping up the pavement with their tombstone
teeth, smashing shop fronts with their wings,
there's nothing in this world that can stop them now.